HORSE & PONY
SHOWS
& EVENTS

HORSE & PONY
SHOWS
&EVENTS

Carolyn Henderson
Foreword by Carl Hester

DK PUBLISHING, INC.
www.dk.com

A DK PUBLISHING BOOK
www.dk.com

Project Editor Maggie Crowley **Project Art Editor** Sharon Grant
Editor Kathleen Bada **Designer** Darren Holt
US Editors Connie Robinson and Sharon Lemon
Managing Editor Jayne Parsons
Managing Art Editor Gill Shaw

DTP Designer Nomazwe Madonko
Picture Researcher Francis Vargo
Jacket Design Margherita Gianni
Production Lisa Moss
Photography Andy Crawford and John Henderson

Paperback Edition, 1999
2 4 6 8 10 9 7 5 3 1

Published in the United States by
DK Publishing, Inc., 95 Madison Avenue
New York, New York 10016
Copyright © 1999 Dorling Kindersley Limited, London

Library of Congress Cataloging-in-Publication Data
Henderson, Carolyn (1955–).
Horse and pony shows and events by Carolyn Henderson. -- 1st American ed.
p. cm. -- (DK riding club)
Summary: A completely illustrated guide to horse and pony shows, competitions, and other events.
ISBN 0-7894-4265-5 (paperback).
1. Horse-shows--Juvenile literature. 2. Horsemanship--Juvenile literature.
[1. Horse shows. 2. Horsemanship.] I. DK Publishing, Inc. II. Series.
SF294.7.H67 1999   98-50743
798.2′4--dc21   CIP
                         AC
Color reproduction by Colourscan, Singapore
Printed and bound in Italy by L.E.G.O.

CONTENTS

FOREWORD

COMPETING IS FUN and exciting. It tests all your riding, training, and horsecare skills – and whether or not you come home with a rosette, it will help you build a winning partnership with your horse. Successful competing depends on the right preparations, whether you are riding at international level, like me, or starting out. This book will tell you all you need to know when you are riding or watching others. It will help you choose the right sport, get your horse fit, and train it so you are confident and safe. Enjoy your reading – and your riding!

CARL HESTER,
INTERNATIONAL DRESSAGE RIDER

WHAT TO ENTER

WHATEVER SORT OF riding you enjoy, you can also compete. There are competitions at all levels to suit everyone from the beginner to the advanced rider, and from the novice horse to the experienced one. Everyone likes to win prizes, but competing is more than that. It allows you to monitor your progress and that of your horse, and have fun at the same time.

Horse and rider in harmony

Half pass an advanced dressage movement

Dressage

Dressage demonstrates the horse's balance and suppleness, the rider's skill, and the communication between horse and rider. Riders perform tests made up of a series of movements, which are judged for accuracy and harmony.

Rider in forward position and in balance with horse

Fly fringes are permitted in the show jumping ring for protection against flies.

Show jumping

Show jumpers need to be balanced and athletic. The riders' aim is to complete a course of fences without penalties for knockdowns or refusals, often against the clock. Puissance competitions have fewer fences and test how high a horse can jump. All horses and ponies can be taught to jump, but some have more natural talent for it than others.

Endurance

This is a fast-growing sport. There are local and international competitions that range from about 20 miles (32 km) to more than 100 miles (160 km). Many riders also take part in noncompetitive pleasure rides of 10–15 miles (16–24 km).

Showing

Showing classes are judged on a horse's or pony's conformation, movement, and ride. A good show horse or pony must be well schooled with good manners. Different countries have different types of show class. Equitation classes focus purely on the rider – the horse is not judged.

Eventing

Horse trials, or eventing, are the ultimate challenge. There are three phases – dressage, show jumping, and cross-country. Top-level three-day events include steeplechase, and roads and tracks phases. Horses must be calm and obedient for dressage, bold for cross-country, and balanced and careful for show jumping.

Top hats are only worn for formal occasions.

Black jacket adds to elegance.

GETTING FIT TO COMPETE

COMPETING IS HARD WORK. You and your horse need to be in good shape. A program of gradually increasing work will develop your horse's strength, suppleness, and stamina. Check that your horse is healthy before you start and that its teeth and hooves are healthy. Ask advice on what, and how much, to feed your horse. Biking and swimming are ways to increase your fitness.

Getting your horse in shape

Getting a horse fit requires different types of work. Hacking, starting with short periods of walk, then increasing to longer, faster rides, builds a horse's stamina and overall fitness. Training makes it more supple and helps build muscle, while gymnastic jumping, or gridwork, makes it more athletic.

Rider works on transitions between paces and large turns to increase horse's suppleness.

A trained horse should work on the bit when it has warmed up, so that it is well balanced and responsive to the rider's aids.

Horse should have active paces.

W

1

3

5

7

If you have little time to ride your pony, knowledgeable parents or friends may be able to help. Lungeing is useful for ponies who are too small for adults; make sure your pony is not lunged more than three times a week, or it will get bored. When lungeing, work on both reins and increase the amount of work from 10 to 20 minutes.

Wear gloves when lungeing.

Side reins encourage pony to accept the bit.

EXERCISE ROUTINE

It is important to keep an exercise routine so you can judge the progress of your horse and spot potential problems. You must also feed correctly; balance forage (grass and hay) with hard feed (grain or pellets). Increase feed gradually; give more forage than hard feed.

ROADWORK	TRAINING & GRIDWORK	HACKING	FEED	CHECKLIST
Walk your horse on level ground for up to 20 minutes a day, building up to 45 minutes. Avoid any hill work.	*Walk should be active and balanced.*	Feed a horse on a ratio of 75–100% forage to 0–75% hard feed, such as grain or pellets.	If your horse is very unfit, extend the amount of walking exercise up to about six weeks.
Introduce short periods of working, rising trot. Do not work at sitting trot. Increase rides out by up to one hour.	Start to train for 15–20 minutes twice a week. Practice different exercises, such as large circles. Introduce canter in week four.	Trail ride four to five days a week. Introduce gradual hill work. Always walk downhill, but ride at a balanced trot uphill.	If in regular work, increase ratio of hard feed to 50%. *A scoop of grain*	Increase the amount of exercise a horse has before increasing its feed, not vice versa. Continue to turn your horse out daily to help it relax.
Basic work to strengthen tendons and ligaments now complete. Horse should have reached basic level of fitness.	Train at walk, trot, and canter three times a week, with short hacks if necessary.	When not training, take longer rides up to one-and-a-half hours. Ride up steep hills if possible.	If necessary, increase feed in line with horse's work.	Check horse's legs daily for signs of injury or lameness. Forage should not be less than 50% of diet for ponies and most horses.
Trotting poles help to improve balance.	Introduce gridwork as part of two training sessions a week. Gradually build up the heights and numbers of fences.	Continue with longer rides, including steep hills. Start fast work, but on ground that will not jar horse's hooves.	Increase feed to peak level, but continue to monitor horse's condition and reduce hard feed if horse is fit enough.	Check fit of saddle. A horse that builds muscle through training will continue to change shape.

CLOTHES AND TACK

CLOTHES AND TACK must be safe, comforta[ble] and suitable for the horse and rider and th[e] type of event they are entering. It is best to get expert advice on fitting tack, and to use equipment such as helmets and body protectors that meet the latest safety standards. Using damaged equipment increases the risk of acciden[ts].

Safety helmet with chin strap

Riding jacket with shirt and tie

Beige jodhpurs

High-top leather boots

WHAT TO WEAR
This rider is dressed properly for general riding in competition. She could enter basic dressage, showing, and show jumping classes. Higher-level competition may require more formal clothes.

Special equipment
Different types of competitions require special equipment. Dressage, show jumping, horse trials, and Western classes all have rules about what the rider and horse should wear.

Safety helmets with colored silks are worn for eventing and long distance riding.

Body protector helps prevent serious injury in the event of a fall.

Flash noseband prevents horse from opening its mouth, giving rider greater control.

Splint boots protect the horse on front and hind legs.

CROSS-COUNTRY CLOTHES
Jumping means that horse and rider need protective equipment. A rider may use different or additional tack, such as a breastplate for control.

Bell boots

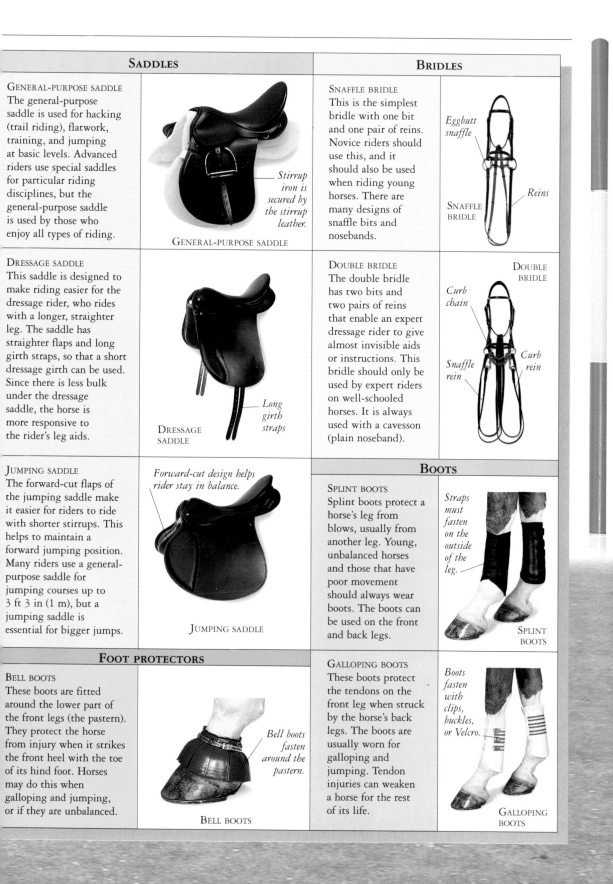

SADDLES

GENERAL-PURPOSE SADDLE
The general-purpose saddle is used for hacking (trail riding), flatwork, training, and jumping at basic levels. Advanced riders use special saddles for particular riding disciplines, but the general-purpose saddle is used by those who enjoy all types of riding.

Stirrup iron is secured by the stirrup leather.

GENERAL-PURPOSE SADDLE

DRESSAGE SADDLE
This saddle is designed to make riding easier for the dressage rider, who rides with a longer, straighter leg. The saddle has straighter flaps and long girth straps, so that a short dressage girth can be used. Since there is less bulk under the dressage saddle, the horse is more responsive to the rider's leg aids.

Long girth straps

DRESSAGE SADDLE

JUMPING SADDLE
The forward-cut flaps of the jumping saddle make it easier for riders to ride with shorter stirrups. This helps to maintain a forward jumping position. Many riders use a general-purpose saddle for jumping courses up to 3 ft 3 in (1 m), but a jumping saddle is essential for bigger jumps.

Forward-cut design helps rider stay in balance.

JUMPING SADDLE

FOOT PROTECTORS

BELL BOOTS
These boots are fitted around the lower part of the front legs (the pastern). They protect the horse from injury when it strikes the front heel with the toe of its hind foot. Horses may do this when galloping and jumping, or if they are unbalanced.

Bell boots fasten around the pastern.

BELL BOOTS

BRIDLES

SNAFFLE BRIDLE
This is the simplest bridle with one bit and one pair of reins. Novice riders should use this, and it should also be used when riding young horses. There are many designs of snaffle bits and nosebands.

Eggbutt snaffle

Reins

SNAFFLE BRIDLE

DOUBLE BRIDLE
The double bridle has two bits and two pairs of reins that enable an expert dressage rider to give almost invisible aids or instructions. This bridle should only be used by expert riders on well-schooled horses. It is always used with a cavesson (plain noseband).

DOUBLE BRIDLE

Curb chain

Snaffle rein

Curb rein

BOOTS

SPLINT BOOTS
Splint boots protect a horse's leg from blows, usually from another leg. Young, unbalanced horses and those that have poor movement should always wear boots. The boots can be used on the front and back legs.

Straps must fasten on the outside of the leg.

SPLINT BOOTS

GALLOPING BOOTS
These boots protect the tendons on the front leg when struck by the horse's back legs. The boots are usually worn for galloping and jumping. Tendon injuries can weaken a horse for the rest of its life.

Boots fasten with clips, buckles, or Velcro.

GALLOPING BOOTS

GROOMED TO PERFECTION

SPECIAL GROOMING and braiding techniques make a horse look its best for competitions. A clean, shiny coat is essential, and braiding and quarter marks show off good conformation. Some breeds, such as Arabians, and Saddlebreds and Quarter Horses, are not shown with braided manes or tails.

QUARTER MARKS
Quarter marks show off the hindquarters. make them, dampen hair and make square diamonds by combin down against the lay the hair. Alternativel use a plastic template

Braiding the tail
Many people prefer braided tails to pulled ones, which have long side hairs pulled out. You can only braid a full tail. Take in just a few hairs at a time and keep your braid tight as you work down the tail.

Start right at the top and keep sections tight for neatness.

Quarter marks

1 Dividing the hairs
Take small sections of hair from each side at the top of the tail. Cross the sections over and take a third from one side of the tail and bring it to the center.

Pass side sections over the center.

Keep hold of the center braid ends so that the whole braid remains tight.

2 Braid down the tail
Bring in small sections from each side and join them with the central braid. Braid down until the center braid reaches two-thirds of the way down the dock.

3 Loop braid under tail
Continue braiding without adding further hair. Loop the end under and stitch in place.

White socks and markings should be spotless.

raiding the mane

braided mane shows off a horse's neck.
ll or shorten the mane to about 5 in
 cm) long before braiding, and thin
f necessary. Although rubber bands
 quick to use, braids sewn with thread
k neater and stay in place longer.

Divide mane into bunches

First dampen mane with water or hair
. Then divide the mane into as many
al bunches as suits the length of the
se's neck. Fasten each bunch with
ubber band.

2 Braid down mane

Braid each bunch,
keeping the braid tight
so that short hairs stay
in place. Double up
the end hairs and fasten
with a band or braiding
thread that is the same
color as the horse's mane.

3 Roll up braid on crest

If using thread, pass
needle through top of braid.
Roll braid up to the crest.
Stitch the braids in place,
or fasten them with
rubber bands.

*Some people
use petroleum
jelly for shine
around eyes
and mouth.*

*Whiskers may
be trimmed
for neatness.*

*Set braids on top
of a thin neck
and to the side
of a heavy one.*

VELL-GROOMED HORSE
ly grooming helps
intain healthy skin and
iny coat. Grease and
t dull the hair. If the
ther is warm, you
y want to bath
r horse before a
npetition. A little
 gloss applied on
ft cloth adds extra
ne for special
asions.

*Take extra care
when washing the tail
of a green horse.*

*Fetlock hair and
hair around
coronet neatly
trimmed*

Hoof oil or polish
should be used only
for shows. Ask your
farrier for advice on
keeping hooves
healthy.

Washing the tail

To wash a tail, stand to one side of
the horse. Wet the hair, then work in
a horse shampoo. Massage the top of
the tail with your fingers to loosen grease
or dirt, then work down the length of
the tail. Rinse thoroughly and repeat if
necessary. Squeeze out the water, then dry
the tail by gently swishing it in circles.

PREPARING FOR A SHOW

START SHOW PREPARATION early; make sure your horse is ready and that your tack and equipment are in good condition. Your horse must be well shod and its vaccinations, or any other documents, must be up to date. Plan ahead; check when your class starts, then work out when you need to arrive at the show.

Preshow preparation

Prepare as much as possible the day before a show. Clean your tack, make sure your clothes are clean, and, if necessary, bathe your horse. You may want to braid your horse the day before if you have an early start. Make a list of things you need to take and get them ready in advance.

Hard hat and gloves

Black or blue show jacket

Stock with tie pin

High-top bo are usually w by older rid Younger ri normally w jodhpur bo

SHOW CLOTHES
For show classes or dressage wear a hard hat and gloves, and either a black or blue jacket with stock and stockpin, or a tweed jacket with shirt and tie. Choose beige breeches and long black boots or short jodhpur boots.

Overgirth worn over saddle in cross-country events

Saddle wi girth, stir and leathe

Long-sleeved shirt for cross-country events

Bridle

Breastplate stops saddle from slipping

Leg wraps for horse

Filled haynet

Wat cont

First-ai for horse

W bu

Tail guard to protect tail while traveling

Cell phone in case of emergency

Studs for shoes

Bell boots

First-aid kit for rider

Splint boots

Grooming kit

Cooler rug

Feed, if needed

Grease – use on horse's legs to help it slide over fences

High-top riding boots

Getting to the show

Allow plenty of time to load your horse and drive to the show. Make sure your horse wears protective traveling gear and a suitable blanket. Check that you have packed all the things you need for the day before loading your horse.

Ramps should have skid-proof surfaces and must be stable and level, to give the horse confidence as it walks up.

Look ahead and calmly lead horse up the ramp.

Leg wraps protect horse's legs while traveling.

Allow extra time for a young or inexperienced horse to settle when you arrive at the show.

Cover up your show clothes or change into them later.

THE TRAILER
Vehicles must be bright and inviting so the horse can see where it is going when loading. There must be enough headroom and each section inside the trailer must be wide enough for the size of horse.

Arrival

Try to arrive at the showgrounds an hour before your class starts. Check that your horse has not gotten hot or injured itself on the way to the show. Find out if classes are running on time, collect numbers, and make entries if necessary. Tack up and walk around until your horse settles down, then warm up lightly.

Stand to one side in case your horse kicks out in excitement.

BEFORE THE SHOW

• Check that horse is shod and its vaccinations are up to date

• Check that clothes and tack are clean and in good condition

• If you have an early start, bathe and braid horse day before show

• Check time of your class so you arrive at the show on time

YOUR FIRST SHOW

YOUR FIRST SHOW is likely to be a small, local competition with classes for novice horses and riders. These classes may include clear round jumping, equitation, pleasure, and trail classes. Shows with dressage tests at beginner level are also suitable. Do not enter more than two classes or your horse may become tired, especially if it is inexperienced.

If your horse is inexperienced you may just want to watch for the first time.

THE SHOWDESK
Go to the showdesk before your class starts, to register and receive your show number from an official. Check how many competitors there are before your turn, so you allow yourself time to warm up. Watch out for other riders in the practice ring, especially near practice jumps. Be ready to enter the show ring when called.

What to expect

At a show, you will see lots of horses, people, and vehicles, and you may hear loudspeaker announcements. Classes are held in areas called rings, and areas where people warm up are called practice rings. Show officials will give you a number to wear and they will tell you when it is your turn to compete.

If riding near parked horseboxes, watch out for other horses being unloaded.

Clear round jumping

Clear round jumping is a good introduction to show jumping for inexperienced horses and riders. You pay a small fee each time you attempt the course, and if you have problems, such as a refusal, you can try again. There is no jump-off, but usually each rider who jumps a clear round gets a special rosette. Think of it as a schooling round, not as a competition.

Rider looks ahead to next jump.

Clear round jumps are low, usually between 1 ft 6 in (45 cm) and 2 ft 6 in (75 cm). The jumps usually include small fillers and easy doubles.

ENJOYING YOUR SHOW

Shows should be fun for you and your horse. You may feel nervous at first, but concentrate on riding and caring for your horse correctly and you will soon feel more confident.

If something goes wrong, try not to panic. Keep calm, and remember that you will always have another chance, and that you and your horse will improve with practice.

	BEFORE THE SHOW	AT THE SHOW	IN THE RING	AFTER THE SHOW
PONY WELL-BEING	Allow plenty of time to load your horse into the trailer and to get to the show, so that both you and your horse are calm on arrival.	Do not ride your horse all day; get off and offer it water often. If your horse needs a feed, allow an hour for digestion before riding.	Stay calm if things go wrong. Do not panic or lose your temper – practicing at home will help you avoid problems next time.	Check that there are no minor injuries or loose shoes. Once back at home, your horse should be calm and comfortable, and not sweating.
HORSE AND RIDER SAFETY	Check that your tack, clothes, and other equipment are clean and in good repair. Horse's shoes must be secure and in good condition.	Beware of excitable horses – do not ride within kicking distance of other horses. Do not ride on pedestrian-only walkways.	Walk calmly into and out of the ring.	Clean tack, clothes, and any other equipment. Check all tack for breakages and send off for repair if necessary.
RIDER MANNERS (ETIQUETTE)	Thank those who have helped you get ready for the show, such as friends and the trailer driver. They will be happy to help you again.	Check in with ring official ten minutes before your turn. Use warm-up ring for your class and do not monopolize the practice fence.	Be courteous to other riders. Observe instructions given by officials. Acknowledge and thank judges where appropriate.	Do not criticise judges' decisions. Avoid temptation to leave muck from trailer at show-grounds. Take all refuse home.

GYMKHANAS

GYMKHANAS, or mounted games, are fast and fun. The word *gymkhana* originated in India; it means a meeting place for equestrian sports. Ponies are better at gymkhana games than horses because they are smaller and easier to turn and to vault onto. Riders have to be as quick and athletic as their ponies.

Mounted games

Balance and coordination are vital when taking part in mounted games. They can be played in teams or as individuals, and include bending races, in which riders have to ride in and out of a line of poles without touching any, and flag races, in which riders place flags in containers while on galloping ponies.

Tent pegging

Tent pegging is a military sport that began in India. An individual, or a team of four riders, carries a 10-ft (3-m) lance and gallops toward a row of tent pegs in the ground. The aim is to push the lance through the ring on the peg and lift it out without slowing down.

Fellow rider holds the pony with its reins in place, ready for the rider to vault on.

Speed and training

A good gymkhana pony has to be as well trained as a top polo pony. It must learn to twist and turn as the rider's body weight shifts, and to turn at top speed. It is important that you do not pull on the pony's mouth, so try to teach the pony to neck rein, so that it turns from the pressure of the reins against its neck, not pressure on its mouth.

...ility and obedience is ...portant for mounted games. ...e pony needs to turn tightly ...und cones, while the rider ...ds to be equally agile to ...y in balance and save time.

The flag race is the gymkhana version of tent pegging.

Long sleeves protect rider's arms from scrapes in case of fall.

Vaulting

Mounting a moving pony is an essential skill for gymkhanas. To vault on, run alongside the pony for a couple of strides and use the momentum of its movement to help push you off the ground as you jump. Swing your right leg well clear of the pony's hindquarters and land in the saddle as lightly as possible.

To vault, practice running alongside your pony with the stirrups flapping. Keep feet clear of irons until mounted.

This pony wears protective galloping and bell boots.

SHOWING

WHATEVER TYPE OF horse or pony you ride, you can enjoy showing. There are classes for different breeds, types, and even colors. Some classes are judged on the horse's conformation, movement, and performance in the ring; others assess the rider's ability. There are also in-hand classes, in which the horse is led rather than ridden. Horses must always be beautifully groomed.

Showing sidesaddle

Sidesaddle classes are judged on either the rider's ability or the horse's conformation and suitability to be ridden sidesaddle. The rider's outfit is called a habit, which consists of a jacket and an apron worn over breeches and boots.

Rider must sit straight and look ahead, not tilt to one side.

Ridden classes

Show horses must be trained and well behaved. In some classes you will be asked to give an individual performance in front of the judge. This means riding your horse to show that it is is obedient in all its paces. Sometimes the judge will ride each horse before deciding on final placings. You may be asked to trot your horse in-hand to show off its movement.

The judge may ask you to ride particular exercises, such as a figure eight.

Standing in a line takes practice. Your horse must be able to stand quietly and to walk away from others when asked.

Riders should we a black, blue, or tweed jacket.

n-hand showing

here are classes for all types of horses and ponies, including young ones, and for different types and breeds. The judge assesses a horse's conformation, so you and your orse must be able to stand still, as well as walk and trot llingly without pulling or hanging back. Your orse must also well behaved th others.

The handler should look neat and be able to control a horse. A hat, jacket, shirt and tie, and beige trousers should be worn.

Walk and trot your horse straight toward the judge to show how it moves.

he judge will ask ders to perform some exercises.

Riding without stirrups shows the rider's balance.

quitation classes

you cannot find a suitable show class for your horse, you have fun in equitation classes. These are judged on the ler's ability, not on the horse's looks. You will be asked to le different exercises, such as figure eights and riding thout stirrups. Competitors may be asked to ride each er's ponies as well as their own.

SHOWING

- The pony and its tack must be spotlessly clean

- Find out if your horse should be shown with a braided mane. Some breeds, such as Appaloosas, are not braided

- Measure your horse, as some classes specify maximum heights for horses and ponies

- Good manners and training are as important as good conformation

DRESSAGE

THERE ARE DRESSAGE TESTS for horses and riders at all stages of training. Tests comprise a series of movements designed to show that the horse is obedient and that the rider uses the correct aids. Beginner level tests include simple movements, such as circles.

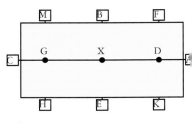

DRESSAGE ARENA
Tests for beginners are ridden in an arena measuring 130 x 66 ft (40 x 20 m). Letters around the arena indicate where a rider should start different dressage movements.

DRESSAGE MOVEMENTS	
20-METER CIRCLE Dressage tests for beginners include the 20-meter circle, which is ridden in trot or canter. The circle can start from A, C, B, or E. Marks are deducted if the circles are squashed or egg-shaped, so ride in a true circle.	20-METER CIRCLE
DOWN CENTER LINE Tests always start and finish by riding down the center line. Be positive as you ride down the line and look where you are going, so that you are able to guide your horse in a straight line.	DOWN CENTER LINE
SERPENTINE LOOPS A three-loop serpentine is one of the most difficult movements in beginner tests. The loops must be equal in size and the rider should ride straight across the center line before starting another loop.	SERPENTINE LOOPS
SHALLOW LOOPS Loops of 10 ft (3 m) or 16 ft (5 m) are ridden down the long side of the arena, between the two outside markers, H and K, or F and M. While riding the loop, horse and rider should maintain a steady rhythm.	SHALLOW LOOPS 16 ft

Turnout

A dressage rider and horse should be clean, tidy, and neat. At beginner level, riders wear either a tweed jacket with a shirt and tie, or a black jacket and stock. Jodhpurs can be beige or white, and boots can be long or short.

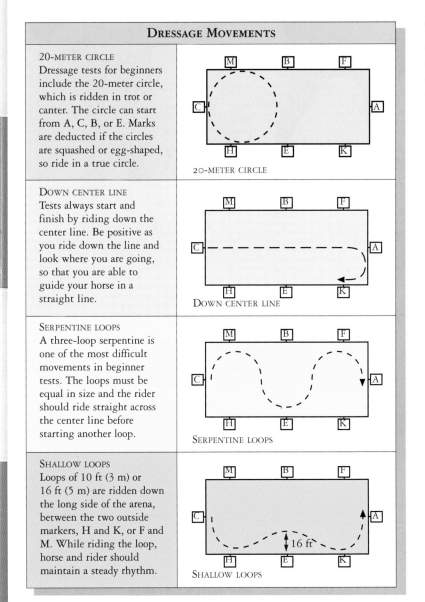

Tails can be pulled or braided. Pulled tails need bandaging to keep them in shape.

Rider creates energy using leg aids, but controls the pace using weight and hands, without pulling back.

Collected paces

At advanced levels of dressage, horse and rider are asked to work in collected paces. When a horse is collected, it is similar to a coiled spring, full of controlled energy. The horse's steps are shorter and higher than in other paces and its hind legs come farther under its body. The rider sits tall and light in the saddle to present an elegant picture.

A braided mane looks neat and helps create a good impression.

CORRECT EQUIPMENT
Riders can carry whips and wear spurs in dressage tests but must not misuse them. Martingales are not allowed but neckstraps, breastplates, and breastgirths are. Only certain bits and nosebands are allowed.

Rider's legs create energy to lengthen stride without increasing speed.

Snaffle bridles are used at beginner level.

Dressage riders should check a dressage rule book to make sure clothes and tack comply with their level of competition. Using the wrong tack will result in elimination.

Hooves are oiled for competition.

Extended paces

In extended paces, the horse's stride should be as long as possible. It is important that the horse stay balanced; it should not pull or lean on the rider's hands. Beginner level tests ask for lengthened strides, which are easier to perform. This is the first step to producing the extended paces of the advanced horse.

DRESSAGE TESTS

A DRESSAGE TEST is a series of movements performed in front of judges to show that a horse is obedient and supple, and that a rider's position and use of aids are correct. Each movement in a dressage test carries up to ten marks. At the end of the competition, the judge gives the riders a sheet with marks and comments about their test. These help riders decide what they need to practice before their next competition.

Rider practices different movements.

LEARNING YOUR TEST
Some people learn tests by drawing diagrams of the movements in the correct order; others walk the test on foot. Practice the movements with your horse, but ride them in a differen order. Do not ride the complete test too many times or your horse may start to anticipate what comes next.

Top-level horses often have braids fastened with white tape.

Dressage riders plan time to warm up, making sure the horse is not too fresh or too tired when it starts the test.

Concentrate on keeping the horse balanced and energetic before entering the arena.

Make sure you know the positions of the letters.

Practice movements that you and your horse are good at. If you attempt movements that you find difficult, your horse may become tense. Concentrate on building its energy and responsiveness.

Bandages used for warming up must be removed before starting the test.

Warming up
There will probably be a special area or ring for warming up at the show. Other riders will also be using the practice area, so be aware of where they are going. Start your warm-up on a loose rein so your horse stretches its muscles. You may need up to half an hour to warm up. Try to stay relaxed, so that you do not make your horse tense.

iding the test

s you enter the arena, look up and smile. Try to keep
our breathing steady to help you stay calm. Make sure
our horse is moving energetically so you ride a straight
ne down the center without leaving the center line. If
ou make a mistake, keep calm – you will have lost marks
r only one movement. Remember to smile and salute
e judge at the end of your test.

Dressage judges look for a horse
and rider that make an elegant picture
together. Movements must be accurate
and performed at the right place.

dvanced horses, such
this, wear double
dles. Beginner-level
rses always wear
affle bridles.

Rider's hands
are sensitive
and do not
pull on the reins.

IN THE RING

- Keep your horse moving
  energetically, but do not rush

- If you perform a movement
  incorrectly, calmly correct your
  mistake, if possible; then
  concentrate on the next movement

- Keep your breathing rhythmic;
  this will help prevent you
  from becoming tense

480

SHOW JUMPING

THERE ARE SHOW JUMPING competitions for ponies and horses at all levels, ranging from small local shows to international competitions. The aim of riding a course is always to have a clear round without knocking down any fences. A course is often ridden against the clock, and the fastest clear round wins. Top level Puissance competitions test the horse's ability to jump great heights, often 6 ft 6 in (2 m) or more.

Splint boots protect the horse's legs when it is jumping.

A body protect should be wor even whe practicin

Distances between jumps for show jumping courses are based on a horse's canter stride measuring 12 ft (3.7 m). Ask advice when measuring distances for a pony.

Novice classes

Novice classes are for inexperienced horses or riders. Fences should be low and there should be no difficult turns or tricky distances between jumps. Clear round classes, in which the aim is to jump a clear round, are an ideal introduction to show jumping. Many shows allow you to attempt more than one round so that you gain extra experience.

SEEING A STRIDE
Learning to ride a balanced, rhythmic canter can help you meet the take-off point for a fence correctly. This is called "seeing a stride." A good way to learn how to do this is to lay a course of poles on the ground and practice riding over them in a flowing rhythm.

Rider looks ahead to the next jump.

Gridwork

Gridwork helps you and your horse become confident and athletic. A grid is a row of fences spaced at the correct distance for a horse's stride. This makes it easier for the horse to find the correct take-off points. The distances are shorter for ponies than for horses. Get an expert to help set up the grid, and always have someone on the ground who can alter the distances if necessary.

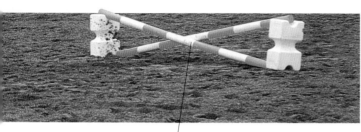

Riding a grid encourages you to improve your rhythm and to ride in a straight line.

Poles are placed at set distances on the ground.

A spread fence encourages a horse to take off correctly and jump in style.

DISTANCES BETWEEN JUMPS
Distances between fences are set to allow a certain number of strides between them. At advanced level, you may need to shorten or lengthen your horse's stride to meet a fence correctly.

An in-and-out, two fences set at a distance, allows one or two nonjumping strides between a fence.

JUMPING FAULTS

- First refusal: three faults
- Second refusal: six faults
- Third refusal: elimination
- Knockdown or foot in water: four faults
- Fall of horse or rider, or both: eight faults
- Failure to go through start or finish: elimination
- Starting round before the bell: elimination

Types of jump

Fences can be uprights or spreads, and a course will have both. Courses will include rustic poles, planks, colored fillers, brush fences, walls, and gates. Advanced courses may have water jumps. Your instructor will help you introduce your horse to different types of fence so that you and your horse approach a jump confidently.

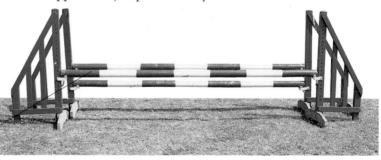

Fillers test horse's and rider's confidence and concentration. Some horses may shy away from fillers.

IN THE RING

WHEN YOU FIRST START jumping at competitions, choose courses that have slightly smaller fences than you jump at home. This gives you and your horse confidence when jumping in strange surroundings. Walk the course carefully, and allow time to warm up before you enter the ring. If you jump a clear round and have a long wait before a jump-off, ride over two or three practice fences just before your turn.

WALKING THE COURSE
Walking the course helps the rider see potential challenges in the ring, such as fences on slightly uphill or downhill approaches. Walk the track you intend to ride so you know which route to take once you are on the horse. In novice classes, distances between combination fences are usually straightforward, but in higher-level competitions distances are more complicated.

A helper adjusts the practice fence by gradually making it taller until it is competition height.

Once your horse is jumping happily, stop. Do not tire a horse before it goes into the jumping ring.

Do not jump a practice fence too many times; six to ten turns is usually enough.

Warming up
Allow about half an hour to warm up before you enter the show ring. First try to make your horse obedient and attentive, then establish a rhythmic canter. Next, jump a few upright and spread practice fences. Practice fences should be no higher than the course you are competing over. Be considerate to other riders in the practice ring.

Riding the course

Enter the jumping ring calmly and set up a balanced canter until you receive the signal to start. Approach the first fence calmly but positively. Always look up and ahead to the next fence; never look back if you hit one, as this will unbalance your horse. As you change direction for each jump, make sure your horse is on the correct lead for canter; come back to trot if necessary. Finally, jump the fences straight on, not at an angle.

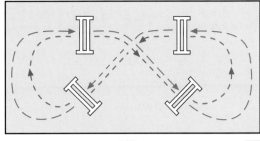

KEY   LONG ROUTE ■   SHORT ROUTE ■

JUMP-OFF

Most jumping classes have a timed jump-off for all riders who go clear in the first round. At home, practice taking a shorter route without spoiling your horse's approach or balance. Making good turns saves more time than galloping between fences, and you will be less likely to hit poles.

*Rider is looking
up and ahead
to next jump.*

*Rider is keeping
light rein contact
that does not
restrict horse.*

Rider is in perfect balance.
She has folded forward from
the hips, and her weight is
absorbed through her knee
and ankle joints.

CROSS-COUNTRY

JUMPING CROSS-COUNTRY fences requires courage from both horse and rider. Fences cannot be knocked down and are tackled at a faster speed than show jumps. If the rider and horse wear correct protective equipment, and if the horse is well schooled, riding cross-country can be safe and fun. Cross-country jumping can be a competition in its own right or part of a horse trial, in which riders also take part in dressage and show jumping.

Jumping technique

To be successful at riding cross-country, a rider must be able to ride fast and remain in control. The rider should maintain a rhythm with the horse's stride so that it meets fences without having to speed up and slow down each time. The rider must stay in balance with the horse even when things go wrong.

Crash helmets and body protectors must be worn to minimize injury if the rider falls.

The red flag must always be on the right as you jump the fence.

Difficult fences

Some cross-country fences are difficult and require careful riding. To tackle a water jump a horse needs power, not speed, so it does not stumble. Drop fences should be approached with energy, but more slowly than ordinary fences. To jump an in-and-out fence, the rider must be balanced, so that the horse lands over one fence and immediately takes off over another without taking a stride.

JUMPING INTO DARKNESS

Jumping into darkness, perhaps from a field into woods, is difficult for a horse. The rider should approach the fence in a straight line, so that the horse can adjust its eyesight to the changing conditions. By sitting up and riding with determination, the rider can control the horse's pace.

...anding in water slows the horse down, */ a controlled approach is vital.*

QUICK ROUTES

On a cross-country course, there is often a choice of routes over single fences, and over combinations with more than one jump. The quicker routes are usually more difficult and are only suitable for experienced horses and riders. If riders are unsure, they take the slower route.

Eventing

Events, or horse trials, are the most challenging of all equestrian sports. Riders have to perform a dressage test, then ride a cross-country course and a round of show jumps. Novice events are run over one day, and intermediate and advanced competitions take place over two and three days. Two- and three-day events include speed and endurance sections over a short course of steeplechase fences, and roads and tracks.

A breastplate helps prevent saddle from slipping back.

Grease on horse's legs helps it slide over fences, thus preventing serious injury.

ENDURANCE RIDIN

Rider and horse must be fit.

COMPETITIVE ENDURANCE rides range from 25 miles (40 km) to more than 100 miles (160 km). There are also noncompetitive pleasure rides of about 10 miles (16 km). Arabians and part-bred Arabians are th most popular types of endurance horse at the top level, but any fit horse or pony should manage shorter distances.

Long-distance riding

Long-distance rides must be completed at set speeds, so riders have to judge the speed of their horses' trot and canter. Riders also monitor their horses' heart and respiration rates to make sure they pass the vet checks along the way.

Support team ensures that horse does not catch a chill.

SUPPORT TEAM
The support team, called the crew, is vital at top level competitive endurance riding. Each rider has a crew to meet up with at various points on a long ride. The crew cools down the horse and makes sure it is comfortable; it also provides the horse with food and water when necessary.

Sloshing down is the safest way to cool down a hot horse. Members of the support team pour water over the horse and walk it around.

Endurance horses are usually allowed to eat and drink small amounts along the ride to help maintain their energy levels.

A fit horse should not get muscle cramps.

The vet will not allow a lame or sick horse to continue.

VETERINARY CHECKS
Veterinarians check horses at "vet gates" – marked stages along the ride. The vets check that heart and respiration rates are correct and that the horse is not lame or injured. A horse that is breathing too fast is not allowed to continue until it has settled.

Bred for endurance

An endurance horse must have strong legs and feet, so that it can cope with long rides. The Arabian has always been a popular breed with endurance riders. It has natural stamina, speed, and agility. Although lightly built, it can carry weight. Anglo-Arabians, part-bred Arabians, and Standardbreds are also popular.

An Arabian has natural balance to cope with difficult terrain.

Horse trails

Organized rides lasting half a day or more are called treks or trail rides. Riders can take their own horse, if it is fit enough, or they can join an organized location trip. Horses need to be sure-footed and sensible, especially on rough ground or in mountainous areas. Riders who enjoy this sort of riding may go on to take part in competitive rides.

PLEASURE RIDES
Pleasure and sponsored rides are organized rides that follow a set route; some include optional jumps. These types of rides are not competitions, but riders may be asked to raise money for a charity. Pleasure rides are a good introduction to long-distance riding for young horses, since they learn to behave in unusual surroundings.

Horses must be agile to cope with mountainous terrain.

RACING SPORTS

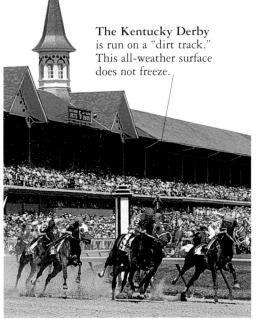

The Kentucky Derby is run on a "dirt track." This all-weather surface does not freeze.

MANY RACING SPORTS are for Thoroughbreds, but there are also special races for Quarter Horses, Arabians, and Standardbreds. Top racehorses are among the most valuable in the world; winners of the world's most prestigious races can be worth millions. Horses can be raced on the flat or over jumps. To train riding or driving horses to achieve racing speeds requires special skill and courage.

Flat racing

Some racehorses are bred to run on the flat. They are backed as yearlings and raced as two- and three-year-olds, but often retire at an early age. Flat racehorses are handicapped by weight according to their age and past performance; this makes races more competitive. Prestigious races include the Kentucky Derby, the Breeder's Cup, and the Prix de l'Arc de Triomphe in France.

Riders that race on horseback are called jockeys.

Jockeys wear crash helmets covered with colored silks.

Steeplechasing

Thoroughbred steeplechasers start their racing careers when they are about four years old. The sport started in Ireland, when two riders raced between two steepled churches. Today the sport is most popular in the British Isles, but also takes place on a small scale in the U.S. and Europe. Famous races include the Grand National in the U.K. and the Pardubice in the Czech Republic.

Steeplechasers jump high, fixed fences at racing speeds over distances of up to 4.5 miles (7 km).

arness racing

andardbreds are bred to trot rather than gallop,
t some reach speeds equivalent to those of
lloping racehorses. Some standardbreds move
eir legs in diagonal pairs, like riding horses,
ile others pace by moving their legs in lateral pairs.

Pacers race by moving
lateral legs together. The left
front and hind legs move at
the same time, followed by
the right pair of legs.

*Goggles protect
a jockey's eyes
from flying
grass and dirt.*

*The groom shifts her weight
to help steer the carriage
around the obstacles.*

*Contestants aim to
complete the course
without knocking
down the balls or
the cones.*

Competitive driving

Competitive driving combines speed with
accuracy. Drivers and ponies race around
a twisting course of up to 20 pairs of
bollards or cones, each pair set just wide
enough apart for the wheels of the carriage
to pass through. Driving trials is another
popular driving sport. Similar to ridden
horse trials, competitors take part in
three phases: dressage, the marathon,
and an obstacle course.

TEAM SPORTS

TEAM SPORTS demand special skills from horse and rider. Polo is one of the oldest and most popular of sports, while polocrosse and horseball have been introduced more recently. To take part in team sports, horses and riders must be in good shape. Riders need quick reactions and good balance for making fast, sharp turns. Team sports are played on ponies and small horses.

Le Trec

Le Trec began in France about 25 years ago, and is divided into three phases. The first is orienteering, in which riders follow a map at set speeds. The second judges the control of a horse's paces. The third involves jumping, cross-country, and dismounted exercises.

The net is used to scoop and throw a soft rubber ball.

Po

Each team has four play whose aim is to score hitting the ball into t opposing team's goal. Play number one attacks, numb four defends, while t other two hold the cent A match consists of four six chukkas, each lasti seven minut

The attacking player must score as many goals as possible.

Polocrosse

Polocrosse teams consist of six players. Each team is divided into two so that only three players from each are allowed on the field at a time. Player number one is the attacker and the only one who can score a goal. Player number two takes the center position, and player number three is the defender. A match is made up of six timed sections called *chukkas*, each lasting between six and eight minutes.

Riders can hook an opponent's stick.

Horseball

Horseball is a relatively new sport that is like basketball on horseback. Two teams of six riders aim to gain possession of a small ball with several handles. Four from each team are allowed on the field at a time, and the ball must be kept in the air. Riders try to take the ball from the opposing team, and then score a goal.

Horseball is played in many countries and is particularly popular in France.

Riders are allowed to "ride off" by bumping into an opponent and pushing them off-line.

Polo ponies are, in fact, horses that stand between 15 hh and 15.2 hh.

Players must always hold the polo stick in their right hand.

HOMEWARD BOUND

WHEN YOU HAVE finished competing, tend to your horse. Before heading for home, cool down your horse and check for minor injuries and loose shoes. Wash any mud from its legs to uncover hidden cuts and remove shoe studs if used. Allow your horse to drink, but make sure the water is not too cold. Once back home, make sure your horse is comfortable before leaving for the day.

Care of pasture horse

At the show, cool down a pastu[r]e horse as you would any other h[orse]. At home, check that the horse i[s] comfortable; it should not be shivering and the base of its ear[s] should feel warm. If necessary, stable and blanket the horse un[til] it is dry and comfortable enoug[h] turn out. Otherwise, turn it out[so] that it can walk around and rol[l]

Rolling helps dry off [a]
sweaty coat an[d]
relaxes the hors[e]

Cooling down

Before going home, make sure your horse has cooled down so that it doesn't get a chill. Walk the horse around, with a blanket on if necessary; it may not need a blanket in hot weather. If it is hot and humid, alternate walking your horse with washing it down until the horse is comfortable.

Muscle cramping may occur if you leave your horse standing still immediately after working hard. Walk it quietly to allow it to relax, and make sure its temperature is stable.

AT HOME

- Check for minor injuries and any heat or swelling in legs

- Make sure the horse has hay and water

- Provide horse with deep bed in its stall, so it can lie down

- If necessary, use extra blankets to keep horse warm

- Always make a final check before you finish for the day

- Check horse for lameness by trotting it first thing the next day

*nload with
*e. A tired
*rse may trip
stumble.

Coming home

Put a blanket on your horse to travel home. A summer sheet is necessary even in warm weather to prevent tired muscles from cramping and as protection from drafts in a moving vehicle. Offer the horse a drink before you leave the show and give it a haynet to help it relax during the journey.

the stall

eck that your horse has traveled well
d there is no sign of injury, sweating,
heat or swelling in the legs. If you
e worried, get expert advice;
eck the horse's legs first thing
e next morning. Put on stable
ankets, then make sure the
rse has hay and water and a
ean, deep bed. If the horse is
y and relaxed, feed as normal.
fore finishing for the day,
eck over the horse, and add or
ange blankets if necessary.

*Give the same quantity
and type of feed as
normal. Clean water
must be available.*

SAFETY AT A SHOW

COMPETING puts extra demands on you and your horse, so it is important to make sure you both stay safe. Use the right clothes and equipment and participate in well-organized competitions only. A veterinarian and qualified first-aid experts should always be available in case of an emergency.

Special grease is smeared on the horse's legs to help it slide over cross-country fences.

Studs come in different shapes and sizes.

Splint boots help preve injury if the ho knocks its legs togeth while jumpin

Bell boots protect the horse's heels.

Cross-countr overgirth fa over saddle.

Rider safety

Always ride with a hat or helmet that meets the highest safety standards. It must fit properly and the harness must always be fastened. If you are jumping, especially cross-country, wear a body protector; this helps prevent injury if you fall. Replace damaged safety equipment and do not buy these items secondhand.

Horse safety

You need to protect your horse when galloping or jumping. Boots are especially important and help prevent leg injuries. They must be the right size and fastened so that they do not slip, but are not too tight. Studs that screw into the shoes help the horse grip the ground.

Wear long-sleeved shirts to keep your arms from being scraped if you fall or ride under branches.

Wear gloves to grip slippery reins and check that the harness on the helmet is fastened securely.

Body protectors have special panels designed to absorb impact if you fall.

Correct ria boots help you your feet safel the stirrup ir

First-aid for rider

All shows should have qualified medical help available. When you arrive at a show, find out where the first-aid station is, in case you need help. If an accident occurs, try not to move an injured rider or remove the person's hat, as this may make back or neck injuries worse. Call the first-aid staff or paramedics, who will know what to do. Always try to keep calm.

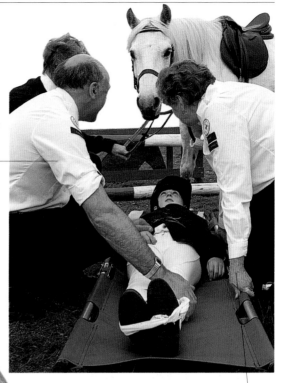

Red Cross volunteers throughout the world are trained to deal with accidents.

Veterinary on call

International competitions have veterinarians in attendance. Organizers of small shows will arrange for a vet to be on call; this means that if a horse is injured, the vet can be contacted and should be there within a short time. Always take a first-aid kit so that you can deal with minor cuts and scrapes.

Always call the show vet for sudden and severe lameness.

Your horse must be protected against tetanus in case of a serious cut or injury.

Trained first-aid staff will know how to prepare an injured rider for transportation to the hospital.

SAFETY CHECKLIST

- When you get to the show, find the first-aid station

- Always make sure your helmet harness is fastened before you get on a horse

- Keep protective boots clean and in good repair. Dirty boots may cause skin problems

- Protective boots cannot be worn for showing or dressage, but you can use them when warming up

- Use studs for competition only, not when riding on the road

MAJOR EVENTS

IF YOU REALLY ENJOY competing, and want to watch the professionals, try to take time to go shows that take place near your home.

This chart lists some of the big equestrian events that you can go to throughout the year, such as show jumping and three-day eventing.

JANUARY	FEBRUARY	MARCH
Taupo Horse Trials, NZ – Three-day event World Cup Show jumping, Sydney, Aus – Show jumping World Cup Dressage, Victoria, Aus – Dressage Tote Warwick Handicap Chase, Warwick, UK – Steeplechase	Florida Classic, Florida – Show jumping Arabian Horse Show, USA – Showing	
At the international Arabian Horse Show in February, a cavalcade of horses and riders compete in multiple disciplines and native costume events.		

JULY	AUGUST	SEPTEMBER
The Tevis Cup, Auburn, California – Endurance Ride Royal International Horse Show, Hickstead, UK – Showing, jumping and dressage	North American Young Riders Championship, Wadworth, Illinois – Dressage, show jumping, and combined training Hambletonian Trotting race, Meadowlands – Trotting race British Jumping Derby, Hickstead, UK – Show jumping Royal Dublin Horse Show, Ireland – Show jumping	The Little Brown Jug, Delaware – Pacing race Burghley Horse Trials, UK – Three-day event Royal Melbourne Show, Victoria – A variety of equestrian events Blenheim Palace Horse Trials, UK – Three-day event Doncaster Races, Doncaster, UK – Steeplechase
For the Tevis Cup, 250 entrants ride over a 100 miles.	The Hickstead Jumping Derby attracts top level riders from around the world. They come to take on the challenge of the renowned bank and Devil's Dyke obstacles.	Burghley Horse Trials is a major event in the three-day event ca European championships are al sometimes held here.

Winners, whether of a large event, such as the National Horse Show, or a small local show, may receive a trophy, and some may even win money.

Riders at top international events and at local shows should always wear clothes that are clean and neat. This helps to add to the overall presentation of horse and rider in the ring.

APRIL	MAY	JUNE
ex Kentucky Three-Day Event, sville, Kentucky – Three-day t	Kentucky Derby, Louisville, Kentucky – Flat racing	US Equestrian Team Festival of Champions, Gladstone, New Jersey – Dressage, show jumping, and driving
yland Hunt Cup, Glyndon, yland – Steeplechase	Windsor Driving Championship, Windsor, UK – Driving Trials	Equitana USA, Louisville, Kentucky – A variety of equestrian events
rajong Endurance Ride, rajong, Aus – Endurance ng	Goodwood Dressage, Goodwood, UK – Dressage	Royal Ascot, Ascot, UK – Flat Racing
Grand National, Aintree, – Steeplechase	Newmarket Races, Newmarket, UK – Flat racing	Golden Horseshoe Ride, Exmoor, UK – Endurance riding
	Badminton Horse Trials, Gloucestershire, UK – Three-day event	British Derby, Epsom, UK – Flat racing
Rolex Kentucky Three-Day t is a proving ground for U.S. s and riders who aspire to pete in international combined ing events.	Known as the *Run for Roses* the Kentucky Derby is the oldest American sporting event. The race is for three-year-olds and is run over the distance of one and one quarter miles.	Equitana USA is the largest international equestrian trade fair and exposition in the US. Held over four days, it features nearly every breed and discipline.

OCTOBER	NOVEMBER	DECEMBER
questrian Team Fall Driving t, Gladstone, New Jersey – age Driving	Breeders' Cup Day, Louisville, Kentucky – Flat racing	National Cutting World Championship, Futurity, Fort Worth, Texas – Cattle cutting
bley Horse of the Year Show, on, UK – Showing	Christchurch Hunter Trials, Christchurch, NZ – Three-day event	
de l'Arc de Triomphe, e – Flat Racing		
Horseball Championship, – Horseball		
grace and beauty of carriages he thrill of competitive driving e captured at the Gladstone Driving Event.		

GLOSSARY

THERE ARE MANY WORDS associated with horses. Some have been used in this book and can be found, with a description of their meaning, below.

AIDS Signals from body weight, legs, voice, and hands that rider uses to communicate with horse. Whips, spurs, and martingales are considered artificial aids.

BELL BOOTS Protective boots to help prevent injury if a horse strikes the heel of a front hoof with the toe of a back one.

BENDING RACE Mounted game in which pony and rider gallop through a row of upright poles.

BODY PROTECTOR Protective garment for rider, designed to reduce the risk of injury in a fall.

BOUNCE FENCES Two fences set at a distance that requires a horse to jump the first, land, then jump the second without a stride in between.

BREASTPLATE Item of gear to help prevent saddle slipping back. Often used for cross-country.

CLEAR ROUND JUMPING Jumping competition for beginner horses or riders where the aim is to jump a clear round over a low course.

COLLECTED PACE A horse is "collected" when it is perfectly balanced and its energy is gathered into short, energetic strides.

COLLECTING RING Area at a show where competitors check in before their class. Maybe used as area to warm up before entering the ring.

CREW Backup team for endurance rider. It meets the horse and rider at stages along the ride to provide food, water, and any help.

DRESSAGE Training; dressage tests are series of movements to show balance, obedience, and athletic ability of horse, and the partnership between horse and rider.

ENDURANCE RIDING Sport which involves riding long distances over set course. Distances range from 25–100 miles (40–160 km).

EVENTING Competition with three phases: dressage, cross-country, and show jumping. Also known as horse trials.

EXTENDED PACES This mean the horse's steps have controlled energy and are as long as possible.

FILLERS Brightly colored, solid inserts in show jumps.

FLAT RACING Races without jumps for two and three-year-old Thoroughbred horses.

GRIDWORK Gymnastic jumping exercises; jumps are set at specific distances to improve horse's athletic skill and confidence, and rider's technique.

GYMKHANA Also known as mounted games; requires an athletic pony and rider.

HARNESS RACING Driving races between horses harnessed to light two-wheeled vehicles called sulkies.

HORSE BALL Sport between two teams; each tries to get possession of a ball with handles to score a goal.

IN-AND-OUT FENCE Two fences in a row with one or two strides between them; distances must be correct for size of horse.

JOCKEY A rider who races horses over jumps or on the Flat.

LATERAL WORK Dressage and training exercises in which horse moves forward and sideways at the same time.

LENGTHENED STRIDES The first stage in teaching a horse to lengthen its paces is to ask for strides that are longer but not faster.

PLEASURE RIDES Noncompetitive rides over distances usually between 16–32 km (10–20 miles).

POLO Fast team sport divided into intervals called chukkas; riders hit polo ball with a stick called a mall to score goals.

POLOCROSSE Team sport that is a cross between polo and lacrosse. Riders scoop up ball with net on the end of a long handle.

QUARTER MARKS Designs made with a brush on a show horse's quarters.

REFUSAL When a horse refuses to jump or runs out to the side of a fence.

REIN BACK Dressage and training exercise in which horse steps backward. The legs move in diagonal pairs.

SERPENTINE Dressage and training exercise in which the aim is to ride loops of equal size and shape – usually three – across the arena.

SHOWING Classes to show horse's conformation, movement, and manners. Can be ridden or walked.

SLOSHING DOWN Technique used to cool down endurance horses. Cold water is poured over the neck, often while horse is on the move.

SPLINT BOOTS Prevent injury if horse strikes one leg with opposite leg or hoof.

STEEPLECHASING Races for Thoroughbred horses over hedges, fences and ditches.

TENT PEGGING Military sport; rider carries 10-ft (3-m) lance and, at a gallop, has to spear and lift peg stuck in the ground.

TREKKING Long, noncompetitive pleasure rides.

VAULTING Jumping onto a moving pony without putting feet in the stirrups. An essential skill for mounted games.

VETGATE Compulsory halt during competitive endurance ride where vet checks horse's soundness, pulse and respiration.

JUMPING PRACTICE

ACKNOWLEDGMENTS

Dorling Kindersley would like to thank the following people whose assistance have made the preparation of this book possible.

The author
Carolyn Henderson has lived and worked with horses for many years. She is a regular contributor to special interest magazines such as *Horse and Hound*, and has written and edited a variety of books on all aspects of keeping, riding, and training horses.

The publishers would also like to thank the following. Hilary Bird for the index, Cheryl Telfer for additional design, and Martin Redfern for editorial assistance.

Lethers, Merstham, Surrey for the loan of equipment and tack. The show organizers and competitors at Chelsham Riding Club Horse Show, Farleigh, Surrey. Jackki Garnham and staff, Beechwood Riding School, Woldingham, Surrey; Sandra Waylett, Gatton Park Livery, Reigate, Surrey; Ebbisham Farm Livery Stables, Walton on the Hill, Surrey, for use of their facilities. The models Holly Clarke, Rosie Eustace, Emma de la Mothe, Kerry Meade, and Alison Forrest.
Also thanks to the horses and ponies used in photography and their owners for loaning them. These are: *Cinnamon Dust* (owned by Holly Clarke); *Eliza Doolittle* and *Ginger Pick* (owned by Sandra Waylett); *Tikki*, *Garochead April*, and *Meliton Bay* (owned by Jakki Garnham).
Every effort has been made to adhere to latest safety standards in the making of this book.

Picture Credits
The publishers would like to thank the following people for their kind permission to reproduce their photographs.

key: *b* bottom, *c* center, *l* left, *t* top, *r* right

Richard Connor/Glen Tanar Equestrian Centre: 38*t*; **John Henderson:** 43*t*;

Kit Houghton: 6-7; 18*b*; 21*b*; 32; 33*b*; 35*b*; 36*t*; 39*t*, *b*; 43*b*; 44*b*; **Bob Langrish:** 2; 8-9; 20*b*; 21*t*; 26*b*; 27*b*; 30*b*; 22*t*; 23*t*; 31; 33*t*; 34*t*, *b*; 35*tl*; 36*b*; 37*t*, *b*; 38*b*; 44*c*; 45*b*; 38-39.

Additional photography
Other photography was taken by **Tim Ridley:** 5*t*; 11*c*, 13; **Bob Langrish:** 11*t*, *c*, *b*; 12*t*;

Useful addresses

Here are the addresses of some societies and other organizations that you may wish to contact.

American Endurance Ride Conference
701 High Street, #203
Auburn, CA 95603
Website: www.aerc.org

American Horse Shows Association
220 East 42nd Street,
New York, NY 10017
Website: www.ahsa.org

The American Polocrosse Association; PO Box 853
Johnson City, TX 78636
Website:
www.ILSweb.net/polocrosse/

American Youth Horse Council Inc.
4903 Iron Works Pike
Lexington, KY 40511
Tel: 800/TRY AYHC

National High School Rodeo Association
11178 N. Huron, #7
Denver, CO 80234
Tel: 800/46-NHSRA

United States Combined Training Association
525 Old Waterford Rd., NW
Leesburg, VA 20176
Website: www.eventingusa.com

United States Dressage Federation
P.O. Box 6669
Lincoln, NE 68506-0669
Website: www.usdf.org

United States Equestrian Team
(and Olympic Training Center)
Pottersville Road
Gladstone, NJ 07934
Website: www.uset.com

United States Pony Club
4071 Iron Works Pike
Lexington, KY 40511
Website: www.ponyclub.org